Original title:
Nurturing Artistic Vision

Author: Annabel Swan
ISBN HARDBACK: 978-9916-87-750-0
ISBN PAPERBACK: 978-9916-87-751-7
ISBN EBOOK: 978-9916-87-752-4

Reflections on the Surface of Imagination

In the stillness of the mind,
Thoughts dance like rippling streams,
Colors swirl and intertwine,
Crafting silent, vivid dreams.

Mirrors echo whispers bright,
Echoes of what could have been,
Fragments glint in soft moonlight,
A tapestry of unseen.

Waves of hope and fleeting doubt,
Ripple across the tranquil floor,
Casting shadows, weaving routes,
To places never seen before.

In this realm where visions play,
Time bends to a gentle sway,
Limits blur and fall away,
As hearts bloom into the fray.

A Garden of Clouds and Colors

In the sky, where dreams take flight,
Cotton puffs of soft delight,
Painting blues and whites afar,
A landscape bright, where wishes are.

Each hue a whisper, each shade a sigh,
Rays of sunlight dancing high,
Petals dropping from above,
Sprinkling earth with youthful love.

Between the storms, a gentle breeze,
Stirs the stillness, makes hearts seize,
A canvas strewn with magic fair,
Of clouds and dreams that linger there.

In this garden where we rest,
Nature's palette, we are blessed,
Each moment a floral song,
In twilight's grasp, where we belong.

Portraits of a Dreamer's Heart

Upon the canvas of the soul,
Brush strokes of longing take their toll,
In vibrant hues, emotions blend,
Each masterpiece a story penned.

Lost in visions, wild and free,
The dreamer paints with ethereal glee,
In shadows deep, and lights that gleam,
Chasing whispers of a distant dream.

The palette speaks of joy and pain,
Of laughter lost and love's sweet gain,
A heart laid bare, in colors bright,
A testament to rich delight.

Each portrait tells a tale profound,
Of journeys vast, where hope is found,
In every stroke, a piece of art,
Reflections of a dreamer's heart.

The Driftwood of Dreams and Art

Washed ashore by time's own hand,
Driftwood curves to form the land,
Stories told in weathered grain,
Echoes of laughter, love, and pain.

Artisans of life’s wild seas,
Shape the wood with gentle ease,
Crafting dreams from tangled knots,
In silence shared, lost in thoughts.

Each piece a whisper, each line a sigh,
A journey from sea to the sky,
In crafted forms, a world reborn,
From fragments tossed, a new dawn sworn.

The driftwood holds the footprints clear,
Of those who dared to persevere,
In every curve, a tale of grace,
In the art of dreams, we find our place.

Serenade of the Senses

Whispers of the breeze delight,
Crickets sing in the soft night.
Moonlight drapes the sleepy trees,
Nature hums, a gentle tease.

Fragrant blooms in gardens grow,
Dancing softly, to and fro.
Tasting rain upon the skin,
Life's sweet chorus, let it in.

The touch of silk on weary eyes,
Echoes of laughter lift the skies.
Bold aromas fill the air,
Memories linger everywhere.

Footsteps trace on morning dew,
Birdsong breaks the dawn anew.
Each moment, a treasure found,
In the senses, joy abounds.

Songs of life in vibrant play,
Guide our hearts along the way.
In this serenade, we blend,
Boundless love, it never ends.

The Dance of Color

Emerald leaves sway in the breeze,
Sunset hues that warm with ease.
Painted skies of orange fire,
Nature’s brush ignites desire.

Lavender fields stretch so wide,
Where dreams and lavender abide.
Golden sunflowers turn their gaze,
Chasing light through summer days.

Silver stars on velvet nights,
Crimson hearts in candle lights.
Colors swirl in life’s embrace,
Every shade reveals its grace.

Azure waves that kiss the shore,
In every hue, we seek for more.
Life's palette rich and deep,
In these colors, secrets keep.

With each stroke, a story told,
In every shade, new dreams unfold.
Join the dance, come take your part,
In the canvas of the heart.

Pages of Possibility

Blank pages wait with eager hearts,
Whispers of dreams, where hope starts.
Pencils poised, ideas flow,
Ink spills forth, a vibrant show.

Each word weaves a tale untold,
Adventures blossoming, bold.
Characters leap from line to line,
In this world, we intertwine.

Chapters filled with joy and strife,
Emotions dance, bringing life.
Stories shaped by hands so free,
Endless journeys, you and me.

Imagination takes its flight,
Guided by the stars so bright.
Every twist a chance to grow,
Through the pages, we will go.

With each turn, horizons shift,
Embrace the magic, the greatest gift.
The story starts with a single pen,
An infinite world, again and again.

Heartbeats of Imagination

In the quiet, thoughts arise,
Dreams take shape before our eyes.
Fleeting visions, colors play,
As the night turns into day.

Whispers stir the silent air,
Creating worlds beyond compare.
Fantasy flows like a stream,
Crafting moments, weaving dream.

Ideas burst like stars at night,
Illuminating future’s light.
Every heartbeat, a spark ignites,
Traveling through the endless heights.

Let them dance upon the page,
Every story, every stage.
With each pulse, the wonders bloom,
Imagination clears the gloom.

So close your eyes and wish for more,
Open doors to worlds in store.
A heartbeat's rhythm leads the way,
To realms where dreams forever stay.

Threads of a Woven Vision

In twilight's gentle embrace,
Threads of dreams softly trace,
Woven patterns of the night,
Whispering secrets in the light.

Colors blend with softest grace,
Silent stories time won't erase,
In every stitch, a glimpse of fate,
Holding truths we contemplate.

Beneath the stars, our hopes align,
Each thread a spark, a chance to shine,
Binding hearts in radiant hues,
A tapestry of vibrant views.

With every weave, a tale unveiled,
In life's fabric, we have sailed,
Stitching moments, pure and true,
A vision woven, me and you.

Through the loom of time we go,
Crafting dreams we long to show,
Threads entwined, we will define,
A future bright, forever mine.

Dances of Light on Paper

In stillness, pencil glides,
Casting shadows, where beauty hides,
Words take flight, like birds in song,
Dancing gracefully, righting wrongs.

Each stroke a whisper, soft and clear,
Inviting thoughts to draw you near,
Illuminated pages glow,
In every line, a story flows.

The ink swirls like colors in air,
Capturing visions, bright and rare,
Sketching dreams with every gaze,
Unfolding tales that set ablaze.

As sunsets kiss the drawn delight,
The paper holds the glow of night,
In the rhythm of a dance so pure,
The heart finds peace, the mind is sure.

With every twirl, creativity sings,
A masterpiece of simple things,
In the quiet, let the light play,
A vivid dance on paper's sway.

Sculpting the Invisible

In silence, visions carve their path,
Shaping dreams away from wrath,
Molding thoughts like clay in hand,
Creating worlds, both strong and grand.

With gentle hands, the spirit flows,
Crafting beauty only it knows,
Invisible forms take solid shape,
In every curve, the mind escapes.

The artist's heart blends with the void,
In each breath, their will deployed,
Through the silence, echoes ring,
Sculpting visions that take wing.

In the shadows, creativity plays,
Chasing light through countless ways,
Creating art where dreams reside,
The mystery begins to guide.

Through chisels bold and gentle hands,
They forge the unseen, make new plans,
Ethereal whispers brought to life,
In the stillness, free from strife.

Ripples in the Pool of Genius

In still waters, thoughts arise,
Ripples dance beneath the skies,
Each idea a droplet bright,
Spreading waves of pure insight.

In the depths, the mind explores,
Unlocking wisdom, opening doors,
Curiosity's gentle sway,
Guiding pathways each new day.

The pool reflects a vibrant hue,
Mirroring dreams that come true,
With every swirl, a thought ignites,
Illuminating countless sights.

Innovation floats like a breeze,
Stirring ripples with subtle ease,
In shared visions, minds unite,
Creating wonders, pure delight.

As the echoes softly fade,
In the pool, foundations laid,
Genius flows like water's song,
In every ripple, we belong.

Brushstrokes of Innovation

Colors collide on the canvas bright,
Dreams take shape, igniting the night.
Ideas dance with a spark so bold,
In each stroke, a story unfolds.

Waves of thought in a vibrant stream,
Crafting the future from a fleeting dream.
With every hue, a vision to share,
In the heart of the creative air.

Textures blend, transforming the space,
Finding beauty in the wild embrace.
Each line whispers of tales untold,
In the brush, the magic unfolds.

Imagination breaks through the gray,
Painting a world where shadows play.
Innovation sparks like a firefly's flight,
In the night sky, a canvas of light.

Brushstrokes march in rhythm's tune,
Creating wonder beneath the moon.
In this art, the boundaries dissolve,
With each creation, we evolve.

The Symphony of Creation

Notes collide in a dance divine,
Echoes rise, and hearts entwine.
Rhythms move with a gentle sway,
In harmony, we find our way.

Strings vibrate with a silent sigh,
Beating drums as time floats by.
Each melody whispers a soulful plea,
In this symphony, we're truly free.

Flutes awaken the dawn's first light,
While choirs soar to the endless night.
In the silence, a heartbeat plays,
Creating magic in countless ways.

Every song tells of hope and pain,
A tapestry woven in joy and strain.
Within the chords, a language grows,
In every note, the essence flows.

Together we rise, in a grand embrace,
Life's symphony, a sacred space.
In creation's arms, we find our role,
In the music, we discover the soul.

Radiance in the Shadows

In the twilight, secrets gleam,
Whispers softly form a dream.
Light and darkness dance in play,
Radiance found in shadows gray.

Flickers of hope in the hidden place,
Illuminate paths we dare to chase.
Each corner holds a tale to tell,
In the silence, we know it well.

Moonlit nights with a tender glow,
Painting the world in whispers slow.
Life emerges from the gentle dark,
Filling the space with a vibrant spark.

Through the veil, we glimpse the light,
Finding comfort in the night.
In every shadow lies a chance,
To embrace life's intricate dance.

From the depths, we rise anew,
In the shadows, we find our view.
Radiance brightens the hidden folds,
With every story, a truth unfolds.

Echoes of the Muse

In quiet corners, whispers flow,
Echoes of the muse, soft and low.
Each thought a drop in the ocean vast,
Collecting dreams from the distant past.

Wings of inspiration take to flight,
Guiding souls through the starry night.
In the silence, a voice so clear,
The whispers of art draw us near.

Fragments of stories drift through the air,
Calling out to those who dare.
Within each echo, a longing stirs,
Opening hearts as the silence blurs.

In every note, the muse will sing,
Crafting wonders, life takes wing.
In the shadows, where visions fuse,
We find ourselves through the muse's cues.

As we listen to the echoes' rhyme,
Time stands still in the fold of time.
Here in the stillness, we find our right,
Guided by echoes, chasing the light.

The Poetry of Creation

In whispers soft, the world was born,
Stars ignited, darkness torn.
From silence deep, a melody,
Nature's song, a symphony.

Mountains rise, with grace and might,
Rivers dance, in silver light.
Each leaf sways, the breeze does play,
Crafting tales in bright array.

Colors bloom in vibrant hues,
Life awakens, with morning dew.
Every creature, great and small,
Contributes to this grand enthrall.

The ocean roars, with fierce delight,
Cascading waves, a wondrous sight.
In every heartbeat, stories weave,
The poetry of life believes.

So let us pause, and take it in,
The wonders vast, where to begin?
In every moment, creation's heart,
An endless work of sacred art.

Echoes of the Heart

In quiet nights, the whispers call,
Memories rise, like shadows tall.
Every heartbeat tells a tale,
Of love and loss, a gentle wail.

Across the years, time softly creaks,
In silence deep, the heart still speaks.
A sigh, a laugh, a tender tear,
Echoes linger, always near.

Through winding paths, we often roam,
Yet in our souls, we find a home.
The moments shared, the bonds we weave,
In echoes soft, we still believe.

The stars above, they twinkle bright,
Remind us of our shared delight.
In every glance, a spark ignites,
The flames of love, our guiding lights.

So cherish well the ties that bind,
For in each heart, a truth we find.
In echoes sweet, we see our part,
The timeless beat of every heart.

Uncharted Realms

Beyond the hills, a horizon glows,
Whispers of dreams where wanderers go.
Through valleys deep, and forests wide,
In uncharted realms, our hopes reside.

With every step, the journey calls,
Adventure waits in hidden halls.
The map is drawn with lines unseen,
In mysteries vast, where we've not been.

A tapestry of tales unfolds,
In every shadow, a truth beholds.
As starlit skies guide our way,
In uncharted realms, we dare to stray.

The winds may shift, the path may bend,
But in the heart, we find a friend.
Through trials faced, we come alive,
In uncharted realms, we freely thrive.

So let us roam, with spirits bold,
In every stride, a story told.
With open minds and open hearts,
In uncharted realms, the journey starts.

The Altar of Imagination

In quiet corners, dreams ignite,
The altar stands, a sacred light.
With whispered hopes and vision clear,
Creation's breath, forever near.

Each thought, a spark, a flame to hold,
In vibrant hues, the stories unfold.
From seed to bloom, the visions grow,
In the altar's space, our passions flow.

Through shifting sands of time and place,
The mind's vast sea, an endless space.
In every shadow, the light shall gleam,
In the altar's warmth, we dare to dream.

With colors bold and brushes wide,
Imagination's tide, we ride.
In every heartbeat, art entwines,
At the altar, creativity shines.

So let us gather, hearts in tune,
Beneath the watchful, silver moon.
In the altar's light, we find our spark,
With imagination's flame, we leave our mark.

Where Ideas Take Flight

In the cradle of night sky,
Thoughts flutter like fireflies,
Dancing on whispers of dreams,
Beneath the moon's soft beams.

Words take off, breaking free,
Soaring on winds of glee,
Chasing clouds, they twirl and spin,
Igniting hope from within.

Sketches of visions form lines,
Painting futures in designs,
Each stroke a chance to arise,
Transcending the mundane skies.

With every heartbeat they rise,
Crafting realms where courage lies,
In the heart of innovation,
Ideas bloom in celebration.

Together, they weave and drift,
An ethereal, boundless gift,
In the quiet, sparks ignite,
Where ideas take their flight.

Shaping Silhouettes

Shadows dance upon the wall,
Figures whisper, rise and fall,
In the glow of fading light,
Silhouettes burn bold and bright.

Every curve tells a tale,
An echo, a soft exhale,
In the dusk, they come alive,
As dreams and hopes collide.

Chiseled lines in shadow's grace,
Frame the wonders we embrace,
Crafting forms from hues once lost,
Every stroke, a measured cost.

Molding thoughts that flicker fast,
Shaping futures from the past,
With patience, art takes its rise,
In shadows, the truth lies.

Together in twilight's breath,
Crafting echoes beyond death,
Each silhouette, an ode of flight,
In darkness, we find light.

Muses in the Mist

Veils of silence drape the morn,
Muses tread where dreams are born,
Through the fog, they softly weave,
Granting visions to believe.

Glimmers twinkle in the gray,
Guiding hearts along the way,
In the haze, ideas form,
A creative, gentle storm.

Whispers echo through the pines,
Carving paths with tender lines,
In the mist, inspiration glows,
As the river of thought flows.

Forms emerge from depth unknown,
In twilight's hush, seeds are sown,
Muses sigh on gentle wings,
In the fog, the soul still sings.

Through the veils of morning light,
Muses dance, a wondrous sight,
In the mist, imagination's kiss,
Unlocks the heart's sweet bliss.

The Undercurrents of Expression

Beneath the surface, currents flow,
Whispers of thoughts too deep to show,
In the silence, voices rise,
Breaking through like hidden ties.

Colors blend in quiet streams,
Carving out the heart's true dreams,
Words paint shadows on the floor,
Revealing truth forevermore.

In hidden depths, the soul takes flight,
Chasing echoes into the night,
With every pulse, emotions churn,
In currents, we yearn and learn.

Fluid shapes, uncharted bends,
Where expression never ends,
Through each struggle, beauty thrives,
The undercurrents shape our lives.

Together, in this woven dance,
We find our voice, we take our chance,
Beneath the waves, we learn to breathe,
In expression, our truths we weave.

Channels of Creative Flow

In rivers of thought, ideas drift,
Like currents of dreams, they shift.
Brush strokes and words, all in a dance,
Imagination's spark, a fleeting chance.

Through valleys of silence, whispers emerge,
A symphony of visions begins to surge.
Ink spills like rain on pages anew,
Each droplet a world, bursting through.

Paths intertwine, a labyrinth wide,
Where shadows and light harmoniously abide.
The muse awakens, a guiding light,
Leading the way through the endless night.

In harmony's embrace, colors collide,
The palette of life, where passions reside.
With every heartbeat, creativity flows,
A river of wonders, forever it grows.

So let your spirit soar and roam,
In channels of flow, you'll find your home.
Embrace the chaos, dance with the muse,
For in every creation, there's much to choose.

The Symphony of Shapes

Lines intersect, a canvas alive,
Geometric specters, in rhythm they thrive.
Circles and angles, a visual song,
In the gallery of dreams, where we all belong.

Squares stack tall, forming the base,
While triangles peak, in elegant grace.
Each form a note, in a grand design,
Creating a harmony, both yours and mine.

Colors collide, a vibrant embrace,
A tapestry woven with infinite space.
Soft curves invite, and sharp corners tease,
In the dance of dimensions, hearts find their ease.

With every stroke, a story unfolds,
In whispers of balance, the magic beholds.
Textures invite, tactile and warm,
In the symphony of shapes, find your calm.

So let the visuals guide your intent,
In the orchestra of forms, find pure content.
For every creation, big or small,
Is a piece of the world, uniting us all.

Fables of the Colorful Mind

Upon the canvas, stories ignite,
In shades of wonder, a vivid sight.
Lilac dreams and emerald skies,
Whispering fables where imagination flies.

Through the garden of thoughts, colors bloom,
Each petal a tale, dispelling the gloom.
Amber dawns and sapphire seas,
Crafting adventures that flow with ease.

In shadows that dance, mysteries dwell,
In every hue, a secret to tell.
Carnelian flames and silver light,
Illuminate paths through the velvet night.

So gather your palette, blend and create,
For tales from the heart, celebrate fate.
With a brush in hand, let stories unwind,
In the fables woven by a colorful mind.

In the theater of hues, let your soul play,
With whispers of wonder, chase fears away.
For in every color, a universe grows,
In the fables of minds, true beauty glows.

Castles of Thought in the Sky

In clouds of dreaming, towers arise,
Castles of thought that touch the skies.
With turrets of wisdom, wide open gates,
Inviting the wanderers to seize their fates.

Bridges of wonder, arching so high,
Connecting the realms where ideas fly.
Each window a glimpse into worlds unknown,
In the gardens of thought, seeds are sown.

Banners of inspiration flutter and sway,
As visions and hopes light up the way.
In this kingdom, creativity reigns,
Where imagination dances, unchained, unrestrained.

Cobbled paths lead to treasures untold,
In the heart of each castle, stories unfold.
With walls made of dreams and roofs of delight,
In castles of thought, we embrace the light.

So dreamers and thinkers, take to the air,
For in every castle, existence is rare.
Let your thoughts soar, let your spirit fly,
In the castles of thought that grace the sky.

Blossoms of Inspiration

In a garden where ideas bloom,
Petals whisper tales of light,
Each thought ignites a spark within,
Encouraging hearts to take flight.

Morning dew on vibrant leaves,
Cleansing doubts, renewing dreams,
With every breath, a chance to grow,
Harvesting hope from sunlit beams.

Colors dance upon the breeze,
Nature's brush paints visions bright,
Every moment, seeds we sow,
In the fertile ground of night.

With open minds, we learn to see,
The beauty in the unseen paths,
Inspiration blooms anew,
Casting aside our echoes and wraths.

So let us tend this sacred place,
Where every blossom tells a story,
In the garden of our souls,
We find our truth, our greatest glory.

Threads of Intuition

Woven into the fabric of life,
Are threads of wisdom, soft and bright,
Guiding our footsteps through the dark,
Sparks of insight, igniting the light.

Each pull reveals a hidden clue,
A gentle nudge, a silent call,
Listening closely, we become aware,
Of the whispers that rise and fall.

In silent moments, we find the way,
Following instincts, trusting our heart,
Unraveling mysteries as we go,
Creating a tapestry of art.

The fabric stitches, rich and strange,
Patterns of life, woven with care,
Embracing the journey, mind, and soul,
Together we breathe the fresh air.

So let us cherish these threads of gold,
Intertwined in our sacred space,
For in each stitch, a tale unfolds,
Connecting us all, a warm embrace.

The Art of Becoming

In every moment, we reshape,
The essence of who we are,
Through trials and triumphs, we learn,
Each experience, a guiding star.

Like clay beneath the sculptor's hands,
We mold our dreams with tender grace,
Embracing change, we rise above,
Finding our own, unique space.

With every heartbeat, life transforms,
A canvas painted with our tears,
Colors blending, creating new,
Reflecting hopes and shadowed fears.

In the dance of fate, we find our way,
Footsteps echo on paths unknown,
Crafting stories, rich and bold,
Each whisper carried, never alone.

So let us celebrate this sacred gift,
The art of becoming, a life profound,
With open hearts, we journey on,
In every heartbeat, love is found.

Mosaic of Dreams

Shards of visions, bright and clear,
Scattered pieces of our soul's flight,
Together they form a grand collage,
A mosaic of dreams, taking light.

Each fragment tells a story bold,
Of hopes and wishes, stitched with care,
Crafted from moments, laughter, and grief,
A beautiful tapestry we share.

Colors merge in harmony sweet,
Reflecting our journeys, proud and strong,
In the chaos, we find our peace,
Resilient hearts where we belong.

So let us gather these shards of fate,
Arrange them in sunlight's warm gleam,
Every piece a note in the song,
Of life's everlasting dream.

Together we create and inspire,
A masterpiece woven by fate's thread,
In this mosaic, we find our light,
Where every dream lives, never dead.

Tapestry of Abstract Reflections

Colors weave through silent nights,
Whispers dance in the twilight's grace.
Thoughts collide like fleeting lights,
Dreams find form in a secret place.

Shadows blend with hues unknown,
Every stitch tells a hidden tale.
Patterns shift, and seeds are sown,
In the heart where visions sail.

Threads of memory intertwine,
Crafted by hands that yearn to see.
Each moment a unique design,
A canvas of infinity.

Echoes resonate in the void,
Fleeting glimpses of life’s embrace.
In this tapestry, none destroyed,
All connected in the vast space.

With every weave, a spark ignites,
Transforming darkness into light.
In the quiet of sleepless nights,
Art is born in silent flight.

Luminescence in the Depths

Beneath the waves, where echoes dwell,
A glow ignites in velvet dark.
Whispers stir as secrets swell,
Painting dreams with a glowing mark.

Rippling currents, gentle grace,
Light dances in an ocean's heart.
In shadows deep, there's a warm embrace,
Guiding souls, igniting art.

Currents trail like glowing threads,
In every pulse, a story told.
Wonders swim where silence spreads,
Unveiling treasures, bright and bold.

Stars emerge from the depths below,
Flickering sparks in liquid space.
They map the paths of ebb and flow,
Lighting dreams that dare to chase.

In the stillness, a breath of light,
Illuminates what's left unseen.
In the depths, the hearts take flight,
In the luminescence, we glean.

The Sculpture of a Starry Idea

In the vastness, a thought takes form,
Carved from stardust and cosmic fire.
Its shape defies the brewing storm,
A vision born of pure desire.

Chiseled dreams in ethereal stone,
Each facet gleams with hopeful light.
In the silence, the seeds are sown,
A future sculpted from the night.

Stars align to guide the way,
Crafting shadows into grace.
Through the void, the echoes play,
As form and essence intertwine in space.

Every curve tells a story bright,
Of the journeys that led to now.
A dance of thoughts ignites the night,
As we shape the stars with our vow.

In artistry, a truth unfolds,
Carved by hands of light and dreams.
The sculpture stands, a tale retold,
A masterpiece of cosmic themes.

Awakening the Sleeping Mind

In quiet moments, thoughts arise,
Flickering sparks in shadows cast.
Unfolding dreams beneath closed eyes,
A world where present meets the past.

Gentle whispers beckon to play,
A symphony of unspoken fears.
Awakening in shades of gray,
Calling forth forgotten years.

Words entwine like ivy’s climb,
Lifting veils from fleeting dreams.
In the stillness, we find the rhyme,
And secrets dance in silver beams.

Awakening streams of thought anew,
Flowing through the corridors vast.
In the chambers, a vibrant hue,
Where the future meets the past.

Mind takes flight on the wings of night,
Chasing stars, elusive, bright.
In that stillness, we see the light,
Awakening to life’s pure delight.

Notes of the Ineffable

In twilight’s grasp, whispers intertwine,
Unseen threads of thoughts divine.
Each moment swells, a silent song,
The heart beats loud, where voices throng.

Through veils of time, shadows dance bright,
A melody weaves in the fading light.
Echoes of truth in the stillness arise,
Awakening dreams in our closed eyes.

Wisdom in silence, the cosmos calls,
Life's tapestry hangs on the cathedral walls.
Amidst the chaos, calm breaths find,
In every heartbeat, the universe binds.

In labyrinths deep, reflections play,
In quiet corners, spirits sway.
Notes of beauty that never cease,
In whispered secrets, we find our peace.

As starlit skies envelop the night,
Fragments of wonder take to flight.
In the sphere of dreams, we dare to roam,
Finding the echoes that call us home.

Dreams Beneath the Surface

Beneath the still, where shadows glide,
Lies a realm where hopes abide.
In the depths, whispers awake,
Tales of joy and hearts that break.

Ripples form in the moonlit pond,
Where memories linger, quietly fond.
Each droplet holds a world inside,
Secrets of wishes we cannot hide.

Bubbles rise, sparkling in ease,
Carrying stories from across the seas.
In the quiet, our spirits dance,
Awash in the echo of chance.

Dreams unfurl like petals blown,
In the silence, our truths are sown.
Roots stretch down, seeking the light,
As we delve deeper into the night.

Lost in the depths, we find our way,
Guided by starlight, come what may.
In the richness of night’s embrace,
We discover hope in a hidden place.

The Essence of Play

With laughter ringing, joy takes flight,
In the heart of day and the hush of night.
Colors blend in a joyous trace,
Imagination gallops in boundless space.

In the corners where dreams collide,
The essence of play is our guide.
Every whisper, a story to tell,
In the dance of whimsy, all is well.

Echoes of laughter, a child’s delight,
In the simple moments, we feel the light.
With every twist, the world unfolds,
In the magic of play, the heart beholds.

Try as we might, we cannot roam far,
For within each heart, there's a shining star.
In the circles we draw and lines we weave,
The essence of play is what we believe.

So let us dance in the evening mist,
Embrace the joy that we cannot resist.
In the rhythm of life, we find our way,
Savoring moments, in the essence of play.

The Pulse of the Creator

In every heartbeat, creation hums,
The pulse of life thunders and drums.
Brushstrokes of time on the canvas unfold,
Stories of wonder and dreams retold.

Through the chaos, inspiration breeds,
Sowing the earth with vibrant seeds.
With fervor ignited, visions emerge,
In the dance of the spirit, we feel the surge.

Wonders abound in the simplest things,
In feathers and stones, the universe sings.
Each star above, a flicker, a spark,
Illuminating paths through shadows so dark.

With whispers of purpose, the creator calls,
In the labyrinth of life, the seeker falls.
Every heartbeat, a language, profound,
In the pulse of existence, connection is found.

As daylight wanes and colors fade,
The essence of life in moments replayed.
In the tapestry woven from all that we share,
The pulse of the creator echoes everywhere.

Embers of Passion in Motion

Fires dance beneath the moon,
Hearts ignite in secret tune.
Whispers blend with shadows deep,
As dreams awaken from their sleep.

Every spark a story told,
Crafting warmth in bitter cold.
Starlit skies share their delight,
In the rhythm of the night.

Time unravels, breathless, free,
Passion flows like the restless sea.
In the chaos, a sweet embrace,
Unity finds its sacred space.

Through the flames, we learn to grow,
Chasing embers' vibrant glow.
Lost in moments, fierce and bright,
We dance together in the light.

A journey weaving love and art,
Passion pulls in every heart.
In motion, we find our way,
Embers guide us, night and day.

The Spirit of Creation Unfurling

Colors bloom in nature's hands,
Where silence speaks and beauty stands.
With each stroke, a tale unfolds,
The spirit's warmth, a treasure gold.

Awakening the dormant seed,
In every heart, a vital need.
Creation whispers soft and low,
Inviting us to dream and grow.

Brush of life against the page,
Turning silence into sage.
Unfurling visions, bright and bold,
An ancient dance that must be told.

In the chaos, forms appear,
Every thought becomes so clear.
Through the lens of hope and grace,
Creation finds its sacred place.

Inspire, ignite, let passions break,
Crafting worlds with each heart's ache.
The spirit sways, a dance divine,
In every beat, art's heart will shine.

In the Arms of Inventive Light

Radiance beams through twilight's veil,
Holding dreams that never pale.
With every spark, we weave our lore,
Inventive light opens the door.

In shadows cast by hopes anew,
We find the strength to break on through.
Moments captured, pure and bright,
In the arms of inventive light.

Echoes linger in the flow,
Guided by a gentle glow.
Curiosity sparks the flame,
Illuminating what we claim.

A canvas rich with hues and shades,
Where every soul a journey made.
In unity, we search and find,
Inventive light entwines the mind.

Thoughts like stars begin to twirl,
In the cosmos, ideas unfurl.
With every brush, a vision takes flight,
Bound forever to inventive light.

Whispers of the Canvas

In silence, artistry awakes,
Canvas breathes, and softly shakes.
Stories waiting to be spun,
Each whisper sparks when day is done.

Brushes dance with graceful flair,
Imprints linger in the air.
Every stroke, a heartbeat's sigh,
Telling truths we can't deny.

Colors sigh in tender breeze,
Unlocking dreams with steady ease.
The canvas calls, “Come, be free,”
Inviting souls to truly see.

Whispers echo, time stands still,
Artistry ignites the will.
In the depths where visions bloom,
A world awakens, chasing gloom.

Through frames of life, we take our stand,
Crafting magic with our hand.
Whispers guide the stroke of fate,
In every heartbeat, art holds weight.

Whispers of the Creative Soul

In shadows soft, ideas bloom,
A whisper speaks, dispelling gloom.
Colors swirl like a gentle breeze,
Crafting wonders with perfect ease.

Thoughts take flight on wings of grace,
Emotions dance, a sweet embrace.
In silence deep, creations start,
Each stroke revealing the hidden heart.

With gentle hands, the canvas sings,
A tale of joy that creation brings.
Dreams ignite in vibrant hue,
Awakening visions, bold and true.

Echoes linger in the quiet air,
In every stroke, a soul laid bare.
From depths unknown, the light breaks free,
Whispers of what is yet to be.

In every heart, a story waits,
Behind closed doors, behind the gates.
So let your spirit freely flow,
In whispers soft, let passion grow.

Brushstrokes of Dreaming Hearts

Across the canvas, visions gleam,
A dance of hues, an endless dream.
With every stroke, the heart ignites,
Filling the world with vibrant sights.

Brush to canvas, breath to life,
In colors bright, we find our strife.
Each hue a tale, both dark and light,
In dreaming hearts, we take our flight.

With gentle strokes, the magic flows,
Beneath the surface, true love grows.
In every layer, a secret told,
A tapestry of dreams unfolds.

The world outside fades into blur,
As passion flows, the spirit stirs.
In this moment, boldly we steer,
Brushstrokes weave the dreams we hear.

Creation’s song is ever near,
In whispered tones, we choose to hear.
So let us paint with all our might,
Our dreaming hearts in shades of light.

The Garden of Imagined Realities

In twilight's bloom, the colors blend,
A garden grows beyond the bend.
In every petal, a dream takes flight,
Where thoughts become the stars at night.

Paths of whimsy twist and turn,
With every step, new tales we learn.
In vibrant hues, our stories play,
A dance of magic, night and day.

Fragrant thoughts in soft embrace,
Each flower holds a sacred space.
With whispered winds, we hear the call,
In sacred gardens, we find it all.

Through fields of wonder, we will roam,
In this vast space, we find our home.
Imagined realms where dreams ignite,
A garden rich in pure delight.

So let us tend this garden fair,
With seeds of hope, we plant and share.
In every dream, a truth revealed,
The garden blooms, our hearts are healed.

Impressions from a Quiet Mind

In stillness deep, thoughts intertwine,
A tranquil space, both yours and mine.
With every breath, the silence grows,
In quietude, the spirit knows.

Each fleeting thought, a gentle brush,
In moments soft, we learn to hush.
Impressions left, like footprints light,
In shadows cast, we seek the bright.

The world outside fades to a hum,
In silence rich, the muses come.
With whispered tones, they softly speak,
In solitude, we find the meek.

A canvas bare invites the heart,
To shed the noise, to play a part.
In every pause, the soul will find,
The beauty kissed by a quiet mind.

So gather close the dreams you weave,
In silent spaces, choose to believe.
The power rests in boundless calm,
Impressions bloom, life's soothing balm.

The Art of Listening

In whispers soft, emotions play,
Each heartbeat speaks what words can't say.
With open ears, the soul can find,
The stories hidden deep, unconfined.

A rustling leaf, a tender sigh,
The world unfolds beneath the sky.
Through silence shared, we come to know,
The power in the love we show.

With patience held, we grasp the truth,
In laughter's light, in shouts of youth.
Listening deeply, we learn to weave,
The threads of life, what we believe.

A gentle gaze, a hand to hold,
In moments still, our hearts unfold.
To hear the soul, let silence reign,
In quietude, we break the chain.

So let us cherish every sound,
In listening, a bond is found.
For in each heartbeat, voice, and sigh,
The art of love will never die.

Celestial Brushstrokes

Across the night, the stars ignite,
A canvas vast, where dreams take flight.
With every twinkle, colors blend,
Transcending time, where spirits mend.

Auroras dance, a painted stream,
A symphony born from a cosmic dream.
In hues of violet, gold, and blue,
The universe whispers secrets true.

Galaxies swirl in cosmic grace,
Each dot of light a timeless trace.
Brushstrokes of fate on the infinite dome,
Our hearts aligned, in this cosmic home.

Constellations tell of ages past,
With shadows cast, our dreams amassed.
Each star a story, each glow a spark,
Guiding us through the endless dark.

In this divine art, we find our place,
Amongst the wonders of time and space.
With open hearts, we paint our soul,
In celestial strokes, we become whole.

Painting the Silent

In quiet corners, colors bloom,
Soft whispers echo, dispelling gloom.
A gentle stroke, a patient hand,
Creates a world where dreams expand.

Each canvas waits for stories told,
In shades of warmth, in strokes bold.
From shadows deep to sunlight's grace,
Art speaks loudly in silent space.

Brush against canvas, wipe the slate,
With every stroke, we navigate fate.
In hues of passion, love reborn,
The heart's palette shows the worn.

Moments captured, stillness found,
In every line, our souls are bound.
The silence breaks with vibrant light,
A masterpiece, a day turned night.

So paint the silent, weave your song,
In strokes of joy, where we belong.
For in each color, life's truth resides,
In art, our spirit forever abides.

Ethereal Journeys

In twilight's glow, our spirits soar,
To realms unseen, an open door.
With every step, the cosmos calls,
In whispered dreams, where silence falls.

Through misty veils, we wander far,
Guided gently by a distant star.
Each breath a journey, light as air,
In ethereal realms, we dare to care.

Time bends softly, moments blend,
On pathways woven, we transcend.
With hearts attuned to the cosmic frame,
In unity, we are all the same.

Between the worlds, we find our truth,
In ageless wisdom, we return to youth.
Exploring realms with open hearts,
Each journey starts where wonder parts.

As shadows fade, our essence glows,
In every thought, our spirit flows.
So take this flight, on wings of light,
In ethereal journeys, we unite.

Seeds of Inspiration in Bloom

In the quiet dawn of spring,
Little seeds begin to sing.
Whispers of the earth below,
Gentle dreams begin to grow.

With the sunlight's golden hand,
Nurtured hopes take root in sand.
Petals stretch to touch the sky,
Colors dance and spirits fly.

Every bloom a tale to share,
Stories woven through the air.
Each fragrance, a memory sweet,
Paths of joy where lovers meet.

Nature's canvas, wild and free,
Painting visions yet to see.
In every leaf, a whisper clear,
Life's adventures drawing near.

As we wander through this maze,
Finding beauty in the rays.
Seeds of thought, in hearts confined,
Bursting forth, our lives aligned.

Kaleidoscope of Inner Worlds

In the depths of a wandering mind,
A kaleidoscope of dreams unwind.
Fragments of thoughts in colors bright,
Twist and turn in the soft twilight.

Mirrors reflecting hopes and fears,
Echoes captured through the years.
Patterns shift with every glance,
Inviting thoughts to take a chance.

Whirling dervishes of light,
Dance together, day and night.
In this realm where shadows play,
Guiding us on a brighter way.

Every twist, a new surprise,
Revealing truths beyond the skies.
Limitless realms of possibility,
Unfolding vast infinity.

In the heart, that secret place,
We find ourselves, we find our grace.
A world that dances in our soul,
Crafting visions that make us whole.

The Alchemy of Thoughts into Art

In the crucible of the mind,
Ideas clash and dreams unwind.
Metals of thought, refined in fire,
Sparkling embers of deep desire.

Each brush stroke, a story told,
Transforming visions into gold.
With every line, our spirits soar,
Alchemy, forevermore.

Casting shadows, etching light,
Creating worlds from day and night.
In silence, whispers take their flight,
Molding shapes, our hearts ignite.

Canvas wide, the heart ablaze,
Inspiration fuels the haze.
From fleeting thoughts, emotions blend,
Art's embrace will never end.

Born from chaos, beauty reigns,
Art reveals what thought contains.
A dance of minds, a clever start,
The alchemy of thoughts in art.

Tides of Creativity Awakened

Under moonlight's gentle sway,
Creativity finds a way.
Waves of thought, they ebb and flow,
In the silence, ideas grow.

With each tide, a rhythm sings,
Bringing forth the wildest things.
Whispers from the ocean deep,
Inspiring dreams that never sleep.

Surfing on those crests of risk,
Catching moments, swift and brisk.
In the splash, a spark ignites,
Illuminating starry nights.

The shore invites us to explore,
Endless realms forevermore.
With every wave, we learn to trust,
Ride the tides, rise up from dust.

Creativity, a boundless sea,
Flowing forth, wild and free.
In the heart, waves softly beckon,
Awakening the dreams we reckon.

The Language of Light

Whispers of dawn glow bright,
Dancing softly in the air.
Colors weave in pure delight,
A melody beyond compare.

Sunsets spill on ocean's edge,
A tapestry of gold and red.
Moments cling like a pledge,
Fond memories in silence wed.

Stars twinkle in velvet skies,
Guiding dreams from afar.
Each spark a child’s surprise,
Wishes carried on a star.

Light bends where shadows play,
Like secrets shared in the night.
A tender hand shows the way,
In the language of pure light.

Through the lens of every heart,
Beauty calls, it draws us near.
From the world, we’ll never part,
In the light, we conquer fear.

Crafting the Invisible

In the stillness, art takes flight,
Whispers of thoughts in the air.
Creating visions out of sight,
Crafting dreams with utmost care.

Shadows dance behind closed eyes,
Colors blend in quiet grace.
Each stroke unveils a disguise,
Fleeting time, a gentle chase.

Threads of hope begin to weave,
Patterns form in unseen light.
In each heartbeat, we believe,
Life unfolds in quiet night.

Minds and hands in harmony,
The invisible comes alive.
With each breath, we aim to see,
In our craft, we dream and thrive.

Behind the scenes, magic brews,
Stories told without a word.
In the silence, we diffuse,
Crafting what is yet unheard.

Shadows and Silhouettes

Shapes emerge as night descends,
Figures dance in twilight's glow.
Silent tales the darkness sends,
In the shade, our thoughts will flow.

Ghostly forms that stretch and sway,
Echoes of what used to be.
In their grasp, the light will play,
Creating space for memory.

Whispers twine and softly tease,
The unknown gently calls our name.
In the voids, we find our ease,
Navigating hopes and pain.

Silhouettes against the moon,
Dancing lightly, lost in space.
In this moment, we attune,
Finding solace in embrace.

Shadows linger, stories spun,
Between the dusk and dawning light.
In their dance, life has begun,
We awaken to our flight.

Breathing Life into Dreams

In the cradle of the night,
Dreams whisper, soft and bright.
With each thought, a spark ignites,
Breathing life into our sights.

Fluttering like wings of fate,
Visions bloom, no need to wait.
Hope cascades in gentle streams,
Nurturing our cherished dreams.

Awakened hearts begin to stir,
With the dawn, we shall confer.
Every heartbeat, every sigh,
Paves the path where wishes lie.

Through the moments, we will tread,
Sowing seeds of what's ahead.
As the sun paints skies anew,
Life unfolds with every hue.

Breathing life into our fears,
Turning whispers into roars.
In this dance of hopes and tears,
We find what our spirit soars.

A Canvas Burst with Possibility

A canvas lies wide, fresh and bare,
Color splashes dance in the air.
Dreams whisper softly, bold and bright,
In each stroke, a spark ignites.

Imaginations paint, unconfined,
Tales of wonder, free in their mind.
Textures blend, a vibrant show,
Every hue tells stories we know.

Brush in hand, hearts intertwined,
The essence of life, colors combined.
Creating worlds, realms anew,
In this haven, passions accrue.

Shapes and shadows begin to play,
In symphonies of joy, they sway.
Each masterpiece a heartbeat's song,
In this space, we all belong.

From chaos blooms a radiant light,
In tender moments, dreams take flight.
With every layer, dreams unfold,
A canvas of life, stunning and bold.

Realms Where Ideas Roam

In quiet corners, thoughts take form,
Ideas gather, a swirling storm.
Whispers linger, soft and wise,
In the stillness, creation flies.

Through clouds of doubt, bright visions break,
In vibrant hues, the mind's awake.
Unbounded realms where echoes soar,
Imagination yearns for more.

Pages turn, with secrets told,
Stories shaping, dreams unfold.
Each notion sparks, a flickering flame,
In this journey, none are the same.

Branches of thought reach high and wide,
As pathways twist, we merge and glide.
A tapestry woven from our dreams,
In realms where possibility gleams.

Together we weave the threads of fate,
Links to the future, creating great.
In the vastness, ideas ignite,
In realms of wonder, we seek the light.

Light from the Depths of Thought

In the caverns of the mind, light shines,
Illuminating the tangled lines.
With every whisper, shadows fade,
In the seeking, bright truths are laid.

Echoes of wisdom from ages past,
Resonate deeply, their impact vast.
As depth reveals its hidden lore,
A radiant glow prompts us to explore.

Thoughts ripple softly, like water's grace,
Reflections sparkling in every space.
In the silence, a brilliance grows,
From the depths, new clarity flows.

Through trials faced, and lessons learned,
A beacon of hope brightly burned.
With open hearts, together we flee,
Towards the light of creativity.

In every stumble, in every climb,
The spark ignites, transcending time.
From the depths, we rise and soar,
As ideas illuminate forevermore.

The Harmonious Dance of Inspiration

In the still of night, a rhythm plays,
A dance of thoughts in gentle sways.
With every heartbeat, passion ignites,
Inspiration whispers, holding us tight.

Echoing softly through valleys deep,
Melodies of dreams, in silence seep.
Brushes, pens, and voices unite,
Creating magic in the moonlight.

Every step feels divinely planned,
As visions bloom, we take a stand.
In this waltz, creativity flows,
A tapestry woven, forever grows.

Through laughter shared and trials faced,
Moments cherished, not to be misplaced.
With every twirl, new paths emerge,
In this dance, we all converge.

With open arms, we greet the dawn,
As inspiration's light carries on.
In harmony, we find our voice,
In the dance, we together rejoice.

Winds of Creativity

In the hush of twilight's glow,
Ideas dance like whispers low.
Breezes carry hopes on flight,
Painting dreams in fading light.

Chasing shadows, bright and free,
Winds entwine with possibility.
Every gust a spark to glean,
In the art of what might seem.

Crafting stories, bold and new,
Each thought a flower, bold in hue.
Blossoms swirl with gusts of chance,
A tapestry in vibrant dance.

Every breath a canvas wide,
Beneath the stars, our thoughts reside.
Caught in currents, swift and grand,
We sculpt our world with gentle hands.

So let the winds of change's call,
Guide our spirits, rise and fall.
In the realm where dreams ignite,
We find our way through endless night.

Sculpting the Abstract

In the silence, clay takes shape,
Fingers mold the dreams we drape.
Textures weave a tale so rare,
Artistry in every flare.

Shadows play on canvas bright,
Colors clash and souls take flight.
With each stroke, a vision grows,
In the heart, the spirit flows.

Patterns form in rhythmic grace,
Crafting worlds, a sacred space.
Ideas merge, collide and blend,
In the hands of time, we mend.

Between the lines, the meaning flows,
Every curve, a story knows.
Abstract visions twist and turn,
In the furnace, passions burn.

Sculpting life from thought to flesh,
In the art, our hearts enmesh.
Through the chaos, clarity lies,
In the abstract, our spirit flies.

In the Garden of Ideas

In the garden where thoughts bloom,
Seeds of wisdom chase away gloom.
Petals soft with colors bright,
Each idea a sheer delight.

Tendrils reach for skies above,
Watered by the rain of love.
Rooted deep in fertile ground,
From silence, inspiration's found.

Buzzing bees and whispering leaves,
Nurtured dreams, the heart believes.
Dewdrops glisten like pure gold,
In this paradise unfold.

Paths untraveled, wild and free,
Journey through creativity.
In the garden, we shall roam,
Finding visions, calling home.

Harvesting the fruits of thought,
In this place, our battles fought.
For in the garden, we shall stay,
Fostering ideas day by day.

Kaleidoscope of Thoughts

In a whirl of colors bright,
Thoughts collide, a vibrant sight.
Fractals twist and patterns bend,
In the chaos, we transcend.

Every turn, new glimpses found,
Voices rise, a joyful sound.
Reflections dance on surfaces,
In this realm, our spirit races.

Through the lens, the world expands,
Ideas float like shifting sands.
Connecting echoes, laughter rings,
In the depth, our hearts take wing.

Moments captured, fleeting fast,
Past and future, fused at last.
In the mirror of our mind,
Kaleidoscopes our truths unwind.

So let us spin in brilliant light,
In the night, our colors bright.
Through this dance of thoughts we chase,
In unity, we find our place.

Wings of a Feathered Perspective

In the sky, a bird takes flight,
Gliding softly, a wondrous sight.
With every flap, it chases dreams,
Life's beauty flows in gentle streams.

From high above, the world looks small,
Mountains rise and rivers call.
Each whisper of wind sings a tune,
Beneath the sun, beneath the moon.

Feathers brush against the breeze,
Dancing lightly among the trees.
Through branches green and skies so blue,
A journey blooms, forever new.

With every gust, horizons shift,
The gift of flight, a precious lift.
In freedom's grace, the heart expands,
Carried forth to distant lands.

Wings of light that soar so high,
Painting canvas of the sky.
In every stroke, a story told,
Life's secrets, bright and bold.

The Palette of Possibility

Colors blend, a vibrant scheme,
Each hue a whisper of a dream.
Brushes dance, the canvas waits,
Stories told through opened gates.

Emerald greens and crimson reds,
Every shade where courage treads.
Golden rays light up the dark,
Painting hope, igniting spark.

The swirls of fate, the strokes of chance,
Texture woven in a dance.
With every splash, a life unfolds,
A tapestry of grace and bolds.

In every corner, visions breathe,
Gather dreams like autumn leaves.
With every layer, the heart takes flight,
In this palette, pure delight.

So dip the brush, embrace the art,
Create a masterpiece from the heart.
In the colors rich and free,
Lies the essence of the soul's decree.

Dreams Woven into Reality

In the stillness of the night,
Dreams take shape, a soft delight.
Threads of silver, strands of gold,
Promises of wonders bold.

Hearts entwined in visions clear,
Whispers echo, drawing near.
With open eyes, we chase the light,
Weaving dreams, igniting night.

Every thought a needle's thrust,
In the fabric, weave our trust.
Stitched with hope and laughter's sound,
In this tapestry, love is found.

Through the quiet, visions soar,
Mapping paths we can't ignore.
From heart to heart, a journey flows,
Into the dawn, where magic grows.

In the dawn, our dreams arise,
Woven into the morning skies.
Each thread a story waiting still,
To bloom and flourish, bend the will.

A Symphony of Color and Thought

Notes of color fill the air,
A symphony beyond compare.
Each brush stroke sings a story bright,
In the soul's embrace, pure light.

Melodies of red, blue, and green,
In harmony, a peaceful scene.
With every hue, emotions blend,
Creating beauty that won't end.

Ideas swirling, swirling fast,
A vibrant canvas, shadows cast.
In the rhythm of paint and sound,
Life’s emotions can be found.

Cadences of laughter, tears in tune,
The palette dances, bright as noon.
In colors bold, thoughts take flight,
Creating visions of pure delight.

Let the colors paint your dreams,
In every hue, the spirit beams.
A symphony of heart and mind,
In this masterpiece, joy we find.

Awakening the Spirit

In the silence of dawn's light,
Whispers of dreams take flight.
Eyes open to the new day,
Hope dances in sun's warm ray.

Gentle breezes, soft and clear,
Embrace every soul held dear.
With every heartbeat, we rise,
Awakening under wide skies.

A journey begins with a spark,
Guided by dreams in the dark.
Strength found in every breath,
Living fully, defying death.

Hands joined in a sacred song,
Together we proudly belong.
Finding light in shared grace,
With joy that we all can trace.

Here in the moment, we stand,
Embracing all with open hands.
Awakening to love’s flow,
In unity, our spirits grow.

Whirlwind of Inspiration

Bright flashes of thoughts collide,
In the whirlwind, we confide.
Ideas dance in vibrant air,
A tapestry of dreams laid bare.

Colors swirl, emotions' flight,
Painting worlds in pure delight.
Voices echo, calling near,
A symphony for us to hear.

Through chaos, the mind ignites,
Creating magic, endless sights.
Fleeting moments we embrace,
Captured time, a sacred space.

Rivers of creativity flow,
Each ripple a chance to grow.
Inspiration, wild and free,
Unlocking what we can be.

Join the dance, let go of fear,
Embrace the whispers, lend an ear.
In the whirlwind, we arise,
A collective of dreamers' skies.

The Alchemy of Creation

In the forge of night and day,
We bend the elements our way.
With passion's fire, visions born,
Turning chaos into form.

Thoughts like gold, we weave and spin,
Crafting worlds from deep within.
Each heartbeat a transformative beat,
In silence, our journeys meet.

From ashes rise the phoenix dreams,
In every pulse, a purpose gleams.
Alchemy of heart and mind,
In the depths, we seek to find.

With hands of dust and love's embrace,
We sculpt the shadows, give them space.
Creation's dance, a timeless flow,
In sacred cycles, we grow.

Through trials, we mold the clay,
In the art of living, we play.
The alchemy of life unfolds,
In every heart, the magic holds.

Threads of the Universe

Woven tightly, fate’s design,
In every heart, the stars align.
Threads of time, each moment's sway,
Binding souls in cosmic play.

Hand in hand, we journey forth,
Discovering the value of worth.
Stitches of destiny intertwine,
In the vastness, we brightly shine.

Colors blend, each story told,
In the tapestry, our hearts bold.
Every loop, a lesson learned,
In the flame, our spirits burned.

Connected by unseen strings,
In harmony, our spirit sings.
Threads of love that never fray,
Guiding us along the way.

In the embrace of night and day,
The universe finds its way.
Together, we weave the dreams,
In the light, our essence beams.

Seeds of Creation

In the soil of silent thought,
Ideas take their gentle root.
Tiny whispers grow so deep,
In the dark, they quietly seep.

Nurtured by the hands of time,
Stories writ in dark and light.
From the seeds, a world shall bloom,
In the heart, dispelling gloom.

Every spark a flicker bright,
From within, a guiding light.
In the garden of the mind,
Endless wonders we shall find.

Growth unfolds with sunny rays,
Colors blend in warm arrays.
Nature's beauty, pure and true,
Sprouts of life in every hue.

Tending to the dreams we weave,
In the quiet, we believe.
Seeds of hope beneath the ground,
In their magic, life is found.

Colors of the Mind

Brush strokes dance on canvassed thoughts,
Vivid hues in tangled knots.
Each emotion paints anew,
With every shade, we come to view.

Reds of passion, blues of calm,
Yellows bright like sun's sweet balm.
Greens of envy, blacks of night,
Mixed together, painting light.

In the silence, colors speak,
Whispers soft yet strong and sleek.
Shapes and forms come into play,
Alive on canvas, bright and gay.

Every stroke, a story spun,
Catching rays just like the sun.
Together, they create a tale,
In whispered breeze, in ocean's wail.

Colors blend in a soft embrace,
Finding beauty in each space.
In the mind where dreams ignite,
A painting of the heart takes flight.

Dreams on the Palette

Across the canvas of the night,
Dreams are born in shades of light.
Each stroke a wish, a journey's start,
Coloring the canvas of the heart.

Brightest stars in deep twilight,
Whisper secrets, pure delight.
In hues of silver, dreams unfold,
In tales of wonder yet untold.

Pinks of dawn in morning's glow,
Awakening the world below.
Every color, rich and bold,
Crafting stories, dreams of gold.

Shadows dance in muted tones,
Echoing our silent groans.
Yet in darkness, colors thrive,
Painting visions, keeping dreams alive.

On the palette, life is cast,
Once a dream, now free at last.
In this blend, we find our way,
Creating beauty day by day.

The Heart's Imagination

In the quiet of the heart,
Imagination plays its part.
Dreams take flight on wings of hope,
Through the stars, we learn to cope.

Stories weave in gentle grace,
Filling time and empty space.
Every thought a spark that lands,
Creating worlds by unseen hands.

Whispers echo, visions swell,
In the heart, we dare to dwell.
To paint our truths, a vivid scheme,
Awakening a radiant dream.

With every heartbeat, tales unfold,
In colors vibrant, rich, and bold.
The heart's imagination glows,
A universe each moment grows.

Let it wander, let it soar,
In love and magic, seek once more.
For in the heart, great worlds ignite,
Fueling dreams in endless flight.

Songs of the Unseen

In shadows lie the whispers,
Of dreams yet to be told.
The echoes of the heartbeats,
In silence, they unfold.

Beneath the moonlit heavens,
A melody takes flight.
The unseen hands of fate,
Guide us through the night.

Each tear a hidden story,
Each laugh a fleeting song.
In the quiet, they gather,
To remind us we belong.

Embrace the weight of journeys,
The paths that twist and wind.
For every note not heard,
A heartbeat is designed.

In the tapestry of living,
Threads of gold and gray.
The songs of the unseen,
Guide us on our way.

Canvas of Compassion

With brushstrokes of kindness,
We paint the world anew.
A palette bright with colors,
Of love in every hue.

The canvas holds our stories,
Each layer, a new try.
In every stroke, a heartbeat,
In every tear, a sigh.

We mingle joy with sorrow,
Create with open hearts.
From every shade of longing,
A masterpiece departs.

In gentle hands, we gather,
The hopes we hold so dear.
A public art of caring,
For all the world to hear.

So let us share our colors,
Let kindness light the way.
In the canvas of compassion,
We find our bright array.

Blossoming Vision

In the garden of our dreaming,
We sow seeds of the mind.
Each thought a budding flower,
In sunlight, they unwind.

With roots that dive so deeply,
Into soil rich and warm.
Our visions break the surface,
In beauty, they transform.

The petals spread like wisdom,
Each color tells a tale.
In the breeze of understanding,
Our spirits will prevail.

As seasons shift and alter,
We nurture growth anew.
In this blossoming vision,
Our dreams will shine right through.

So tend the thoughts like flowers,
Let passion be the rain.
In the garden of our vision,
The world will know our name.

The Voyage of Creativity

Set sail on waves of wonder,
With colors as our guide.
In the boat of inspiration,
We journey far and wide.

Through storms of doubt we travel,
With courage as our sail.
Each stroke a breath of freedom,
In our hearts, we will prevail.

Across horizons gleaming bright,
Where new ideas arise.
In the voyage of creativity,
We chase the endless skies.

Harbors filled with visions,
A compass made of dreams.
In every turn and tempest,
Our spirit gleams and beams.

So let the tides inspire us,
To craft, to build, to play.
In the voyage of creativity,
We'll find our truest way.

The Birth of Ideas

In quiet whispers, thoughts arise,
The seeds of dreams, beneath the skies.
A fluttering spark ignites the mind,
New worlds await, waiting to be signed.

From shadows deep, a vision clear,
Breath of inspiration, drawing near.
Crafting echoes, hearts entwine,
In every dream, the stars align.

With every stroke, a canvas blooms,
Infinite paths as vision looms.
The dance of colors, bold and bright,
Painting life in strokes of light.

In silent chambers, wonders grow,
Fleeting moments often flow.
Each echo builds a vibrant sound,
In the mind's eye, hope is found.

So let them soar, let them be free,
These whispered thoughts, our legacy.
For in the birth of every dream,
Lives the essence of what we deem.

Illuminated Pathways

Beneath the moon, on winding ways,
We wander through the night's soft haze.
With every step, the shadows dance,
Guided by stars, we take our chance.

Paths uncharted, secrets unfold,
A tapestry woven, stories told.
Each flicker shines with whispered grace,
A journey drawn in time and space.

In gentle light, the world appears,
Casting away our doubts and fears.
Each step we take, a choice we make,
Creating dreams, with hearts awake.

The night's embrace, a soothing balm,
With every breath, the night is calm.
We navigate through veils of dark,
Finding hope in every spark.

Together we walk, side by side,
In illuminated paths, we glide.
With every moment, a chance to see,
The beauty in life's mystery.

Spilled Ink on Paper

With quill in hand, and heart in tow,
The ink flows freely, thoughts will grow.
Each word a thread, weaves tales anew,
A journey shared, just me and you.

The paper waits, a silent friend,
In every line, our souls we send.
Stories twist, as time stands still,
Reflections of love, pain, and will.

Through valleys deep and mountains high,
Adventures penned beneath the sky.
Moments captured in every stroke,
A world exists in words we spoke.

The whispers linger, echoes fade,
In pages worn, our dreams are laid.
With every tear, a journey spun,
In spilled ink, our hearts are won.

As chapters close and new begin,
The tale extends, alive within.
In every letter, dreams take flight,
Spilled ink becomes our guiding light.

Embracing the Unknown

With open arms, we face the dark,
Venturing forth, igniting the spark.
The mystery calls, a siren's tune,
In the heart of night, beneath the moon.

With every step into the vague,
We shed the past, unchain the plague.
Lessons learned in shadows cast,
Forward we march, unbound and vast.

The winds of change whisper loud,
Ushering in the brave and proud.
Unfurling dreams, like sails at sea,
In the unknown, we dare to be.

Not every path is mapped or planned,
Yet in uncertainty, we understand.
The beauty lies in what we find,
In every twist, a chance to bind.

So here we stand, hearts in the fray,
Ready to dance in wild ballet.
For in embracing all that's new,
We find the strength to break on through.

Fables of the Mind

In the garden of thought, ideas bloom,
Whispers of wisdom from shadows loom.
A labyrinth of feelings, twists and turns,
In every corner, a lesson yearns.

Masks worn in silence, truth hides inside,
Echoes of stories where secrets reside.
Through pages of memory, we wander still,
Chasing the wonders that time cannot kill.

Fables narrated by stars up above,
Crafted in laughter, stitched with love.
Each tale a thread in the tapestry wrought,
Of experiences gathered, lessons taught.

The mind, a canvas, with colors so bright,
Painted with dreams that dance in the night.
From sorrow and joy, each stroke is defined,
Creating the fables that stir in the mind.

So weave your own stories, let them unfold,
In the fabric of life, let your heart be bold.
For every fable is yours to ignite,
A beacon of hope in the depth of the night.

The Essence of Expression

Words like raindrops, gentle and clear,
Falling on silence, a song for the ear.
Each phrase a dance, a moment to share,
In the essence of life, we lay ourselves bare.

A brush of emotion, colors the page,
Each line, a heartbeat, a glorious stage.
From whispers of love to the echoes of pain,
In the essence of expression, all is regained.

Stories entwine like vines in the sun,
Binding our spirits, making us one.
Through laughter and tears, we find our release,
In the essence of expression, we discover peace.

Let your heart speak, let your soul shine,
In the shadows and light, let your truth align.
For the essence of life is found in the voice,
In the beauty of words, we find our choice.

So let each expression be free and design,
A path to understanding, where hearts intertwine.
In the dance of our voices, we rise and we blend,
The essence of expression, on it we depend.

Tapestry of Whispers

Threads of the night weave stories near,
Whispers of shadows drawn soft and clear.
Breezes that carry a lover's sweet sigh,
In the tapestry of whispers, moments fly by.

Each secret a stitch, in silence they blend,
Creating a narrative that twists and bends.
In the fabric of dreams, soft shadows take flight,
A tapestry woven in the heart of night.

Echoes of laughter, the weft of delight,
Stitched with the memories that shimmer so bright.
Each whisper a promise, a bond to maintain,
In the tapestry of whispers, love is the grain.

Gentle and woven with threads of the past,
Stories emerge, in the present they last.
In the warmth of the silence, we find what we seek,
A tapestry vibrant, through whispers we speak.

So let every murmur be cherished and heard,
In the tapestry woven, let love be the word.
For through gentle whispers, connections ignite,
Crafting a masterpiece, cloaked in the night.

Luminescent Dreams

In the stillness of night, dreams softly gleam,
Whispers of hope in a silvery stream.
Stars flicker gently in the velvet expanse,
In luminescent dreams, we dare to dance.

Visions awaken in a twilight haze,
Coloring shadows, igniting our gaze.
Through ethereal realms where our spirits soar,
In luminescent dreams, we long for more.

Each heartbeat a rhythm, a pulse in the dark,
Guiding our journeys with a luminous spark.
In the tapestry woven of wishes and schemes,
Our hearts write the stories of luminescent dreams.

So follow the light that the night has bestowed,
Through chambers of mystery, where love is owed.
In the glow of the moon, with each breath we take,
We find our reflection in dreams we make.

Embrace the enchantment, let fears drift away,
In the glow of our visions, forever we'll stay.
For in luminescent dreams, we are free and alive,
Awakening worlds where our aspirations thrive.

The Quiet Power of Art

In shadows deep where colors blend,
Whispers speak, they never end.
Canvas holds a silent song,
In every stroke, we all belong.

Brushes dance with gentle grace,
Life and dreams they interlace.
Each hue a voice, a tale unfurled,
Art unveils a hidden world.

Through stillness blooms a vibrant fire,
Filling hearts with pure desire.
A silent echo through the years,
Artened with joys and hidden fears.

Beauty found in soft embrace,
Time suspends in this sacred space.
Each masterpiece a journey shared,
In quiet power, we are bared.

From silence sounds the loudest call,
In every line, we rise and fall.
A journey deep with every part,
In the quiet power of art.

Chords of Inspiration

Notes linger in the evening air,
Creating dreams from whispers rare.
Strings resonate with heart's delight,
Chords of hope ignite the night.

Harmony weaves through dusk's embrace,
Melodies guide us in their grace.
Each rhythm a stepping stone,
Inspiration feels like home.

A symphony of thoughts combine,
Transcending time, they intertwine.
With every beat, our spirits rise,
In music's warmth, true joy lies.

Echoes dance on timeless shores,
In every sound, new life restores.
The heartstrings play a vibrant tune,
Painting dreams beneath the moon.

With chords that reach both far and wide,
In melodies, we find our guide.
Each note a spark that lights the way,
Inspiration blooms every day.

Beyond the Veil

Where shadows play and secrets hide,
A world awaits on the other side.
In twilight's glow, the veil is thin,
A dance of souls, where life begins.

Beyond the veil, the whispers call,
Echoes of memories, rise and fall.
In stillness, visions may unfold,
A tapestry of stories told.

With open hearts, we venture near,
To places filled with dreams sincere.
Each glimpse a truth, a fleeting light,
Guiding us through the endless night.

Transcending realms where shadows blend,
Connections forged that never end.
A bridge between the worlds we tread,
In unseen paths, by spirits led.

Beyond the veil, we come alive,
In sacred spaces, we revive.
The dance of life, a timeless quest,
Where every soul finds peace and rest.

The Introspection of Canvas

Colors clash in layered thought,
Within the canvas, battles fought.
Each stroke a whisper of the mind,
In silent corners, truths we find.

Canvas bears the weight of dreams,
Reflecting life in vibrant themes.
With every hue, introspection grows,
A journey deep where wonder flows.

In solitude, the brush reveals,
Emotions pointed, cutting peels.
A mirror held before the eye,
Where fears and hopes blend as we try.

Each layer tells of days gone past,
Imbued with memories that hold fast.
Through turmoil and through gentle grace,
We find ourselves in this sacred space.

With every work, a voice is born,
In chaos or in quiet morn.
The introspection of the heart,
In every piece, we take our part.

Breaths of Inspiration

In every whisper, dreams take flight,
Ideas shimmer in the soft moonlight.
With every heartbeat, hope ignites,
A tapestry woven through starry nights.

Through valleys deep and mountains high,
The spirit dances, and the heart does fly.
In the silence, voices rise,
Crafting new worlds beneath the skies.

Each sigh a spark, each glance a clue,
The canvas of life, painted anew.
With every pause, a thought unfolds,
Stories of wonder longing to be told.

In shadows cast, a light appears,
Chasing away the weight of fears.
In the spaces where thoughts collide,
Magic springs forth, an endless tide.

Breathe deep, embrace what’s yet to come,
Let your heart beat like a drum.
For in each breath, a world we weave,
Inspiration found, if we believe.

Flourish in the Realm of Ideas

In the garden of thoughts, seeds are sown,
Each idea sprouts, uniquely grown.
With colors bright, they intertwine,
Creating visions, vast and divine.

Like branches stretching towards the sun,
Each moment cherished, each battle won.
Cultivating dreams with care and grace,
Nurturing visions, a sacred space.

In whispers soft, guidance is found,
Where imagination flourishes, unbound.
From every corner, brilliance blooms,
Filling the air with sweet perfumes.

Like rivers flowing, ideas cascade,
Winding through hearts, a vibrant parade.
With every pulse, creativity flows,
In the realm of thought, the spirit grows.

Beneath the sky, where wonders thrive,
The essence of brilliance is kept alive.
So take a step, let your heart steer,
Flourish in realms where hopes appear.

Constellations of Creativity

In the tapestry of night, ideas gleam,
Like constellations forming a dream.
Each flickering star, a tale to tell,
Of journeys taken and hearts that fell.

With stardust woven in every thought,
Galaxies flourish, new paths are sought.
Through cosmic dance, visions unite,
In the vast expanse, igniting the light.

Each nebula whispers a secret sound,
Echoes of genius, profound and round.
With every insight, new worlds expand,
Creativity held in a nurturing hand.

As comets blaze a trail through the dark,
Ideas ignite with a vibrant spark.
In the universe of mind and soul,
Constellations thrive, making us whole.

Embrace the cosmos, reveal your sight,
In the darkness, seek the light.
For in every dream, a star is born,
A tapestry of brilliance, forever worn.

The Embers of Imagination

In the glow of dusk, ideas flicker,
Softly igniting, ever quicker.
With each ember, a story starts,
Creating warmth in wandering hearts.

Through the haze, the past remains,
Whispers echo with subtle refrains.
From ashes rise, new visions bright,
Crafting pathways bathed in light.

In the fires of thought, dreams are spun,
Lighting the way, one by one.
Each spark a promise, a chance to learn,
In the heart's embrace, passions burn.

Like a forge where steel meets flame,
Imagination shapes, igniting the same.
Through every challenge, the flames will grow,
Turning the embers into a glow.

So let your thoughts dance, let them play,
In the twilight, chase shadows away.
For in each ember, a world ignites,
Crafting tomorrows from yesterday's nights.

Vibrant Echoes

Colorful whispers fill the air,
Dancing softly without a care.
In the heart, melodies play,
Guiding us through the vibrant day.

Echoes of laughter, bright and bold,
Stories of youth and wonders told.
Every moment, a tune so sweet,
In this symphony, life feels complete.

Shadows linger, but they fade,
As vibrant colors start to invade.
With every heartbeat, joy will rise,
Painted hues beneath the skies.

In gardens blooming, dreams take flight,
Illuminating the dark with light.
Harmony flows in every sound,
In vibrant echoes, love is found.

So let your spirit freely roam,
In every echo, we find our home.
With open hearts, we create,
A world that's vibrant, never late.

Chasing the Light

In dawn's embrace, shadows retreat,
Morning whispers, fresh and sweet.
Golden rays break through the night,
Chasing dreams into the light.

With every step, hope intertwines,
In the glow, our spirit shines.
Paths illuminated, less the fright,
Guided onward, chasing light.

Clouds will gather, storms may rise,
Yet in darkness, courage lies.
Through the struggle, visions ignite,
Fearless in our chase for light.

At sunset's blush, we find our trace,
Every moment, a sacred space.
With hearts ablaze, we reunite,
Forever bold in chasing light.

So let us run, hand in hand,
To places bright, a promised land.
In every dawn, a new delight,
Together always, chasing light.

Capturing the Unseen

In quiet moments, secrets dwell,
Hidden wonders, stories to tell.
With gentle hands, we reach inside,
Capturing what the heart can't hide.

A fleeting glance, a tender smile,
Magic lingers, if just a while.
In shadows cast, truths abide,
Woven softly, like the tide.

Through fleeting time, our memories blend,
In whispered thoughts, we find a friend.
To see the unseen, we must believe,
In every smile, in every weave.

With eyes wide open, we shall find,
The beauty hidden, intertwined.
In silence speaks what words can't say,
Capturing dreams that drift away.

So take a breath, and slow the pace,
Embrace the moment, every trace.
To capture all that lies between,
The heart that beats, the unseen scene.

Reflections of the Soul

In still waters, secrets lie,
Mirrors of dreams, beneath the sky.
Each ripple whispers, soft and true,
Reflections echo, me and you.

In the twilight, shadows play,
Chasing remnants of the day.
Within the depths, emotions swirl,
Capturing life in a gentle whirl.

Every heartbeat, a story told,
In depths of longing, love unfolds.
A dance of light, a sacred scroll,
This is the mirror of the soul.

With open eyes, we seek to learn,
Through every turn, our passions burn.
In quiet moments, find your role,
Embrace the beauty of the soul.

So dive within, let silence speak,
To find the strength within the weak.
For in reflections, we are whole,
Together, always—reflections of the soul.

Visions in Bloom

In gardens where the colors play,
Petals whisper secrets of the day.
Sunlight spills on emerald leaves,
Nature's canvas, magic weaves.

Breezes carry sweet perfume,
Butterflies in graceful flume.
Every bud a story tells,
In this realm where beauty dwells.

Morning dew on blossoms bright,
Kissing dreams awake with light.
Moments captured, fleeting yet,
In a dance, we won’t forget.

As shadows stretch, the day will fade,
Yet in our hearts, the memories laid.
Each bloom reflects a whispered prayer,
Visions linger in the air.

Tonight the moon will softly gleam,
A silver thread, a gentle dream.
In the quiet, hope will rise,
Visions bloom beneath the skies.

Unfolding Mysteries

Beneath the surface, secrets lie,
Whispers held in voice of sigh.
Branches twist with stories old,
Nature's tales waiting to be told.

The night reveals its starry cloak,
Veiled shadows, tales unspoke.
In silence, echoes softly blend,
Mysteries begin to transcend.

Crimson dawn, a path unfolds,
A journey into unknown holds.
Every step a choice we face,
In the labyrinth, time and space.

The heartbeats of the world align,
Threads of fate in stars that shine.
In the weave of night and day,
Unfolding mysteries lead the way.

With every turn and every glance,
Life's enigma invites us to dance.
Hold the wonder, face the fear,
In every moment, truth draws near.

Strokes of Genius

In quiet corners, thoughts take flight,
Colors blend, a symphony bright.
With every brush, a story flows,
A masterpiece the spirit knows.

Ink spills dreams on pages wide,
This canvas where emotions ride.
From silent screams to gentle sighs,
Art reveals where passion lies.

With strokes bold, the heart displays,
A world shaped in subtle ways.
Imagination knows no bounds,
In creation, freedom surrounds.

Voices echo through the night,
From shadows forms embrace the light.
Each creation whispers truth,
Strokes of genius capture youth.

In every line, a heartbeat blends,
The artist's soul that never ends.
Through painted dreams, we find our place,
In colors' dance, we embrace grace.

The Order of Chaos

In swirling winds, the world will bend,
Patterns form where lines transcend.
Beneath the chaos, whispers gleam,
A rhythm found in every dream.

Fragments dance in wild array,
Harmony hides in disarray.
From tangled thoughts, we must evolve,
In the mystery, we resolve.

The universe spins, star dust flies,
In chaos rests the subtle ties.
What seems a mess, a wild spree,
Can lead us to the harmony.

Every clash a chance to grow,
In the turmoil, seeds we sow.
Through the fire, we learn to thrive,
In the chaos, we come alive.

Embrace the storm, let worries fade,
Within the tempest, strength is laid.
The order lies in wild release,
In every chaos, find your peace.

The Atlas of Untold Stories

In shadows deep, where secrets dwell,
Whispers trace, like stories to tell.
Maps unfold in hearts that yearn,
Each line a journey, each page a turn.

Fragments lost in time's embrace,
Hopes and fears find their place.
Every tale, a thread of gold,
Woven gently, never old.

Through valleys vast, and mountains high,
Silent echoes, a gentle sigh.
Paths unseen, where dreams collide,
In this atlas, souls abide.

The ink of life, a vibrant hue,
Illuminates all we pursue.
A compass drawn from love's design,
Maps of fate, eternally entwined.

With every story, a heartbeat starts,
Resonating deep within our hearts.
Each untold tale, a spark that glows,
In this atlas, the spirit flows.

Mosaics of Memory and Emotion

Fragments glimmer, a dazzling sight,
Each piece tells of day and night.
Colors blend in a vibrant dance,
Crafted moments, a fleeting chance.

Shattered dreams, yet still they shine,
In the chaos, stories entwine.
Layers rich with laughter and tears,
A tapestry woven through the years.

Echoes linger in quiet halls,
Whispers of love, the heart's own calls.
In every shard, a tale unfolds,
Memories precious, more than gold.

Restless spirits, they twist and twirl,
In the mosaic, they rise and swirl.
Each emotion, a brushstroke bold,
In this canvas, stories told.

From sorrow's depths to joy's ascent,
A reflection of what we represent.
Mosaics of life, a radiant glow,
In every heart, a story flows.

Cultivating the Seeds of Expression

In the garden of thoughts, we sow,
Seeds of ideas, waiting to grow.
Watered by dreams, nourished by heart,
In fertile soil, each plays a part.

Whispers of longing, rustle the leaves,
In the silence, the soul believes.
Cultivating passions, wild and free,
Harvesting words, like a fragrant tree.

Tending to feelings, both tender and raw,
Embracing the gaps, the light, and the flaw.
Each bloom a moment, each petal a phrase,
In the garden of time, we find our ways.

With each season, new colors ignite,
Expressions evolve, taking flight.
In the cycle, we learn and renew,
As seedlings of thought break through the dew.

The harvest is more than what we perceive,
In every expression, we dare to believe.
Cultivating dreams, our spirits expand,
In the garden of life, we make our stand.

A Journey through Uncharted Dreams

Across the horizon, where shadows fade,
Lies a path where dreams are laid.
Every whisper guides the way,
Into the unknown, we boldly sway.

With stars as guides and hearts aligned,
The canvas of night, our fears unwind.
Through valleys low and mountains steep,
In this journey, we take the leap.

The air is thick with possibility,
In every heartbeat, a vivid thrill.
Uncharted lands, where courage grows,
In the realm of dreams, anything goes.

Through storms that rage, and skies that clear,
We find our strength, we silence fear.
With every step, horizons blend,
In this journey, we transcend.

Awake to visions of worlds untold,
With open hearts, we will be bold.
Together we'll wander, hand in hand,
Through uncharted dreams, a wondrous land.

Echoes of a Wandering Muse

In quiet corners, whispers grace,
The muse dances, time can't erase.
Chasing dreams on winds of night,
Ink flows freely, heart takes flight.

Echoes linger, softly say,
In every step, a new ballet.
Thoughts awakened, colors blend,
Artistry grows, there is no end.

Through shadows cast, a path is drawn,
A story told from dusk till dawn.
With every stroke, the canvas sighs,
Creating worlds, where passion lies.

Each heartbeat fuels the flame's embrace,
In the silence, I find my place.
With every breath, possibilities gleam,
The wandering muse, a timeless dream.

Canvas of the Unseen

Brushstrokes whisper, colors collide,
On canvas stretched, visions abide.
Shapes emerge from depths unknown,
A tapestry of thoughts, but alone.

Eyes closed tight, imagination flows,
In silent realms, where beauty grows.
Each hue a story, told anew,
In the quiet, dreams come true.

A palette rich, life's shades explored,
In every corner, beauty stored.
The unseen dances, freely sways,
On canvas bright, in countless ways.

Artistry speaks without a sound,
In whispered tones, the heart is found.
Creating worlds where none exist,
A canvas blooms, in colored mist.

Illuminating Shadows of the Mind

In the corridors of thought, they play,
Shadows dance, in shades of gray.
Illuminated by gentle light,
The whispers of dreams take flight.

Behind closed eyes, visions gleam,
Every shadow, a lost dream.
Fragments linger in the air,
Illuminating secrets bare.

Thoughts entwined in twilight's veil,
Chasing echoes, a silent trail.
With every flicker, truth reborn,
From darkest depths, a new dawn.

In quiet whispers, wisdom flows,
The mind reveals what it knows.
Through shadows deep, I will explore,
Illuminated thoughts forever soar.

Harmonies Hidden in Silence

In the stillness, music awakes,
A symphony of heartbeats, no fakes.
Whispers of wind, a soft refrain,
In silence deep, echoes remain.

Notes unspoken, together they weave,
A harmony crafted, if one believes.
Emotions blend in the quiet air,
From hidden depths, melodies flare.

Listening closely to the soothing sound,
Life’s serenade can be found.
In moments shared, solace blooms,
Within the silence, a heart resumes.

So let the quiet be your guide,
With every breath, let feelings glide.
In the shadows, where dreams ignite,
Harmonies hidden bring pure delight.